Alongside of the Lijiang River there is a mountain, which looks like a snail from a distance. It is called Snail Peak. A touching story of this mountain has been passed down over hundreds of years.

1

Once upon a time, there lived a hard-working young man named Shihan. Everyday after returning from the fields he would cook a meal for himself.

One evening, on his way home, he happened to see a snail dying of thirst on the beach.

Out of pity Shihan took the snail home and put it into a large water jug.

The next day Shihan went home for supper. The moment he opened the door he saw there, on the table, a steaming-hot meal that smelled delicious.

"Who's so kind as to cook for me?" Shihan wondered. Since he was hungry he ate it at once without second thoughts.

The same thing happened for several days. "What's this all about?" he asked himself. Suddenly an idea came to his mind, which he thought would reveal the secret.

The next morning, acting on his idea, Shihan pretended to go to the fields, but actually he hid behind the house. A moment later, he heard some noise coming from the house. It was a beautiful girl emerging from the water jug.

Everything became clear. He tiptoed into the room and put
the lid on the jug before he expressed his thanks to her.

"That's nothing, compared with your saving my life," she said shyly. "I don't know how to thank you enough. My name is Snail. Seeing that you're hard-working and honest, I'm willing to marry you."

From then on the young couple lived happily. Snail not only wove skillfully, but could also read, paint and recite poems. Once in a while she even taught Shihan to read and write or to sing.

After several years three lovely children, Baibai, Heihei and Daidai, were born. Each one was prettier than the other.

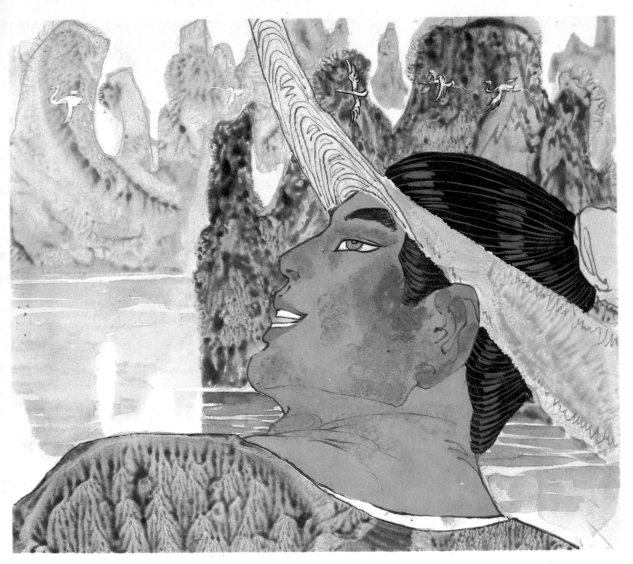

One day Shihan, who was usually very quiet, sang while working in the fields. This surprised the secretary of the magistrate, who was passing by on a spring outing. "Who taught you, a simple farmer, to sing?" he questioned Shihan.

"My beautiful wife," replied Shihan. "She can also paint and write poems," he added proudly. "Incredible," the secretary thought. He followed Shihan home, hoping to find out.

Here the secretary met Snail. To test Snail's ability he sang,
"The carp in the picture is reddish and fresh, but tell me how
many scales it has." "Well, tell me how much your eyes are
worth since they are so sharp?"

Seeing himself no match for Snail, the secretary bowed his head and said again and again, "Wonderful, wonderful." And then he left.

Back in the county office, when speaking to the magistrate, the secretary praised Shihan's wife to the sky for her beauty, virtue and intelligence.

On hearing this the magistrate desired to possess the beautiful and talented woman. He said, "Go tell Shihan to ask his wife to cook ten dishes for me."

The next day the magistrate was dumbfounded when he saw Snail, a woman of dazzling beauty. But the dish of leek with scrambled eggs made him angry. "I told you to fix ten dishes, why only one?" he shouted.

"This is leek (which in her language sounded the same as 'nine')," Snail said calmly. "Leek with eggs means nine plus one. That makes ten, doesn't it?" The magistrate went away, speechless.

When out of the house, the magistrate, with one foot on the
stirrup, thought of a new idea and said, "Young lady, am I
mounting or dismounting?" With one foot inside the thresh-
old and another out, Snail retorted, "Am I going out or
coming in?"

Nothing could beat Snail. Flying into a rage from shame, the magistrate said to Shihan, "Give me a rope made of straw ashes tomorrow, or I'll take your wife as my concubine."

"How can I make a rope out of ashes?" asked Shihan. He was really worried. Snail calmly made a rope out of straw.

When the rope was ready, it was burnt and became a straw-ash rope. "Go and tell the magistrate to come for the rope," Snail urged her husband.

Of course, a straw-ash rope cannot be lifted. This made the vicious magistrate furious. He retaliated by saying, "You succeeded this time, but I won't spare you unless you bring me a cock's egg within three days. If you don't, your wife will be mine."

This worried Shihan almost to death. "Don't worry, I'll take care of it," Snail comforted him.

Three days later the magistrate, still self-confident, came to Shihan's home. "Shihan," he shouted loudly, "bring me the cock's egg now."

"No shouting," Snail said as she came out of the house. "Don't you know Shihan is delivering a baby inside?" "Rubbish," the magistrate cursed, "how can a man bear a baby?" "Right you are," responded Snail. "Since men cannot have babies, cocks cannot lay eggs!"

Completely beaten, the magistrate ordered his men to seize
Snail. At that instant, Snail rushed into the house, took down
the scroll on which a carp was painted, and together with her
husband and children she fled through the back door, and to
the Lijiang River.

The magistrate and his men were in hot pursuit along the river bank. Opening the scroll, Snail begged, "Sister Carp, please take us away."

The Red Carp, with its tail swaying, jumped into the river, carrying Snail's family towards the opposite bank.

Utterly annoyed, the magistrate ordered his men to take a
bamboo raft and go after Snail's family.

On and on, and with great effort, the Red Carp carried the Snail family away. In the dim light of the dusk, the torches of Snail's pursuers could be seen in the distance.

As the bamboo raft got closer and closer to the Red Carp, the magistrate ordered his men to shoot arrows.

At this crucial moment, Snail patted Shihan on the shoulder and he turned into a silvery frog, which then dived into the water.

A rumble was heard and Snail turned slowly into a snail-shaped peak.

Seeing this, the magistrate and his men turned pale with
fright. They were just about to flee when a carp appeared on
the surface of the water. With water gushing out of its
mouth, it created a turbulence which turned the bamboo raft
over.

Since then, along the Lijiang River there rises the magnificent Snail Peak with three huge snail stones nearby. Not far from it, there can be seen the Silvery Frog Stone and the Carp Peak from which flows a waterfall that irrigates all the fields around.

First Edition   1986

Hard Cover: ISBN 0-8351-1322-1
Paperback: ISBN 0-8351-1323-X

Copyright 1986 by Foreign Languages Press

Published by Foreign Languages Press
24 Baiwanzhuang Road, Beijing, China

Distributed by China International Book Trading Corporation
(Guoji Shudian), P.O. Box 399, Beijing, China

Printed in the People's Republic of China

CHINESE FOLK STORY

Shihan and
the Snail

Adapted and Illustrated by
Jiang Zhenli

FOREIGN LANGUAGES PRESS   BEIJING